How to Make Money on EBay

Learn How to Start Selling on Ebay and Make Money Online

Introduction

Hello! Firstly, thank you for taking the time to purchase and read my book.

This will be an amazing adventure for anyone who is serious about making money on EBay!

Let me tell you about myself, or initially, let me tell you a little about what I am not. I am not a ghost writer, I am not a millionaire (yet), I am not an internet marketer who sells books on things I have never done.

I am a UK based entrepreneur, who has a real current EBay business amongst other businesses. EBay was one of my first successful ventures, and I learnt some amazing (little known) tips along the way that I will share with you in this book.

My plan is not to fill your head full of wishful get rich quick schemes, but to teach you how, with a little work you can easily replace your income or create a full time (or more income) from a very small investment. I promise not to hide anything from you or pretend to be something I am not. This is a real honest account and guide of starting an EBay business and exactly what and how to do it.

Yes it takes some work (especially in the beginning), Yes you will have setbacks, Yes you will want to throw your computer through a window (maybe that was just me??) but in the long run it's worth it, Join in the adventure with me in an easy step by step plan!

All of the underlined words in this interactive book are clickable links. They will take you to the site or resource you need. If you are using an older model kindle that does not support browsing to read this book, I would suggest downloading the kindle app or kindle reading software for your phone, pc or tablet when you come to start to take action on this book. This way you always have access to the necessary links etc.

© **Copyright 2014 by Stacey Berriman- All rights reserved.**

This document is geared towards providing exact and reliable information in regards to the topic and issue covered. The publication is sold with the idea that the publisher is not required to render accounting, officially permitted, or otherwise, qualified services. If advice is necessary, legal or professional, a practiced individual in the profession should be ordered.

- From a Declaration of Principles which was accepted and approved equally by a Committee of the American Bar Association and a Committee of Publishers and Associations.

In no way is it legal to reproduce, duplicate, or transmit any part of this document in either electronic means or in printed format. Recording of this publication is strictly prohibited and any storage of this document is not allowed unless with written permission from the publisher. All rights reserved.

The information provided herein is stated to be truthful and consistent, in that any liability, in terms of inattention or otherwise, by any usage or abuse of any policies, processes, or directions contained within is the solitary and utter responsibility of the recipient reader. Under no circumstances will any legal responsibility or blame be held against the publisher for any reparation, damages, or monetary loss due to the information herein, either directly or indirectly.

Respective authors own all copyrights not held by the publisher.

The information herein is offered for informational purposes solely, and is universal as so. The presentation of the information is without contract or any type of guarantee assurance.

The trademarks that are used are without any consent, and the publication of the trademark is without permission or backing by the trademark owner. All trademarks and brands within this book are for clarifying purposes only and are the owned by the owners themselves, not affiliated with this document.

Table of Contents

Chapter 1: The Course 7
Chapter 2: The Beginning... 10
Chapter 3: What to Sell & Where to Get Them... 20
Chapter 4: Making EBay Easier 30
Chapter 5: Building the Business 39
Chapter 6: Building Your Online Brand and Business Beyond eBay 43
Chapter 7: Avoiding Common Online Business Mistakes 62
Chapter 8: Money Magnet Mindset 77
Lastly... 89

Chapter 1: The Course

Ok, so you want to make money online.

Most people who decide to take this leap either have a young family, larger outgoings than incomings or hate the grind of the 9 to 5 and want more freedom. Whichever group you fall into or whatever your personal reasoning is, it has led you here. Everyone reading this book has one common goal in mind, to use the big old web as a way to create a substantial reliable income. Some of you may have some experience with the world of online retail, others may know nothing, but what we aim to do in this book is take the seed of an idea and help you grow it into a money tree.

When people decide they want to start a business online, they have a few options to name a few: Blogging, Marketing and Information Marketing, Web Services and Retailing. I personally at some point or another have dipped my toe into all of these online ventures (or adventures as I like to call them) and made money from all of them (some more than others) but the one I found most lucrative personally was retail. This is because there are so many great platforms already out there to work with; the hard work is already done! I know many entrepreneurs who make their living solely from EBay. No messing around with web designers and marketing your website. EBay already has millions of daily visitors, visiting with one intention, to buy something!

Don't get me wrong, having a website, blogging, marketing, social media marketing etc, they are all fantastic ways to grow a business, and I do briefly talk about these in the last section of the book, but it's important to get a solid foundation in place for your business, using a platform that will carry on making sales even if you don't do any marketing for a few days, and best of all I am going to show you how lots of it can be automated and some tips that only a handful of people are aware of!

Obviously if you have ended up here you have an interest in selling on EBay. But let me briefly talk about the benefits of starting an EBay business. Firstly, you don't need a lot of money to invest to start an EBay business. I started my first EBay business with just £250, and I have known people start theirs with £25. It's easy and simple to use, you don't need any major computer skills. The traffic generation is done for you, buyers flock to EBay every day without you spending a penny on marketing! Also, a massive chunk of the business can be automated. Meaning you can literally sit back and watch the sales come rolling in! Lastly, my favourite part; if you have the IPhone EBay app and stay logged into it, every time you make a sale your phone will KERCHING! Ok ok, that's maybe not so important, but trust me, it never gets old, that sound still makes me dance!

Ok, so are you ready to get started? Follow the simple steps in this book and you can be earning money in no time!

If you have some experience with EBay you may not use the first few steps, but please ensure you read through them as you may pick up a few tips you didn't know.

Here is an overview of the course:

1) Registering Your Seller Account
2) Importance of Feedback and Your First Feedback
3) Listing a First Item
4) Deciding What to Sell and Research
5) Sourcing
6) Professional EBay Presence
7) Listing Your Inventory
8) Automation
9) Achievement on EBay
10) Increasing Margins
11) Scaling up

Chapter 2: The Beginning...

Step 1: Registering Your Seller Account

Many of you will already have EBay account (In fact I won't spend a lot of time talking through this step as I assume most of you will or know how to go about opening one), but for those of you who are totally new to <u>EBay</u> don't worry-Signing up is very simple. Please follow the simple steps below:

1) Go to <u>EBay</u>.

2) In the top left corner you will see an option to sign in or register- click the register and fill in the online form. You will be sent an email to confirm your account.

3) You will also need to open a PayPal account to buy or sell. To do this visit <u>www.paypal.com</u> – You will find their sign up button at the top right. You will need to follow the instructions to add a bank account and debit card which will then allow you to pay for items and get paid for items.

4) Once you have set up your account, you will want to register as a seller, to do this, just click sell at the top toolbar and EBay will take you through the steps. (Please be aware positioning of these links can change depending on what device you are working on) I would suggest just signing up as a personal seller for now- we will talk more about the pro options later in the book.

5) Spend some time familiarizing yourself with the EBay platform, click on every link under the "My EBay" section so you can see what each part does. You probably will not use all of the tools available to you, but it's handy to know what is there. Some of these options will change when you sign up for a business account or shop also, so I recommend repeating this step after you reach that stage.

Step 2: The Importance of Feedback & Your First Feedback

EBay's feedback system is the backbone of EBay. It compromises of three components; the Comment the positive, negative or neutral rating and the Detailed Seller Rating (or DSR) as its better known. Both are equally important for different reasons.

The comment and the positive, negative or neutral are what your potential customer will see. Many perspective buyers will look more at how many positive feedback's you have rather than scroll through all the comments, but if you are a relatively new EBay seller, they may well do this to ensure you are a reliable seller. The early days are the most important when it comes to feedback, because, when you have a few thousand feedback, you can hide the odd negative or neutral, but this is not the case when you don't have many positives.

The DSR is anonymous, so you will not see which buyer leaves which rating here; you will just see how many stars you are rated by all of your buyers. They choose between 1 and 5 stars for your service in the areas of: Accurate Description, Seller's Communication, Dispatch Time, and Reasonable Postage Costs.

EBay use these DSR's more than your feedback to determine your performance, so much so that if you make a certain level of Power Seller and have very good DSR performance you get a discount on your fees. We will talk more about this in a later chapter, but it's worth keeping this right. It has not been confirmed by EBay but there are some people who believe EBay's algorithms for your ranking in the buyer search use DSR's as an element to an extent.

You do not want to go into selling with no feedback what so ever, so what I would like you to do next is to browse EBay and purchase 5 items (they do not have to be expensive items- you can even buy products from China for less than 50 cents) The aim of this is that the sellers will leave you some feedback and it gives you a number next to your name which looks better to potential buyers.

Step 3: Listing Your First Item

For the purposes of learning how to sell items, I want you to begin by digging out a couple of items from you attic or garage that you no longer use that you can sell. The purpose of this is firstly to familiarize yourself with the EBay selling forms, but secondly, it will get you a couple of feedbacks as a seller.

Ok, no now you have your item. Let's look at how to list the item.

1) Login to you **EBay** account

2) On the top toolbar, click Sell

3) If you're item has an EAN or ISBN (Basically a barcode number which is a product identifier) you can type it into the search box to see if it's listed in EBay's catalogue. This is a great tool for items like DVD's and books as it will add generic information you can then add to. So if you have one of these enter it an click search and select your item from the search results- if you're item is not on the list you will need to add all information manually as in 4.

EBay have recently made it criteria that all items selling on their site have unique product identifiers for business sellers. Do not panic, you can buy these very cheaply on the site itself.

4) If you do not have a number or your item was not listed in EBay's catalogue then simply type the name of your item that you're selling into the search box to find suggested categories.

5) Select the category which best suits the item you are selling and click continue.

6) Your title is the most important part of your listing. Do not simply put "necklace for sale" as there are hundreds of necklaces for sale on EBay and you don't stand a chance of

appearing at the top of EBay's best match search with this. Think about the aspects of your necklace and what you would search for if you were looking to buy it. Then include these keywords in the title. For Example: "Vintage Silver Heart Necklace, Beautiful Antique Necklace with Crystal Heart Locket"

This title includes multiple short keywords people may search for such as: necklace, silver necklace, heart necklace etc. but it also includes long tail keywords that people may search for such as: Vintage Silver Heart Necklace, Antique Necklace, Crystal Heart Locket.

These keywords are part of what EBay uses to rank your item based on relevance to what people are searching for.

When you come to start selling products for profit you will also list benefits in the title, for example if you sold slimming pills your listing title might be "Slimming pills. Lose Weight with high quality weight loss tablets, FREE diet plan with every diet pills purchased."

So in this title we have included keywords such as slimming pills, weight loss tablets and diet pills, but we have also covered benefits such as lose weight and free diet plan. This will attract more buyers.

Now for long titles like this you may need to use the subtitle feature, but this does cost extra money and in the beginning I would suggest using one less benefit and just using the main title until you have built up some return on your initial stock investment.

7) Select your condition

8) Add your images. Now your images are your second most important aspect of your listing. Your images should be well lit (taking them on your smart phone is fine) and the subject of the image should be in the center of the image. You should also make sure you upload it the correct way up (sounds obvious but I have seen it!) and that you take photos from multiple angles or using its different functions if applicable. For example, some hoovers have a hand held vacuum that clips off. You would want to take a photo of the full hoover and the hand held vacuum.

Also ensure if your item has any faults that you photograph these. The aim is not to hide things from the buyer- we want good feedback remember, but to be totally honest. So if you're tent has a small hole in the ground sheet, make sure you mention it in your description as well as take a photograph- of course when you upload your photo's you want the photo that looks the best as the one that appears first- so make sure you upload that one first so that your image attracts more buyers to view the item.

9) Fill in the buyer specifics if you're item is a specific brand etc.

10) Your description, many people believe this is the most important component of the listing. I disagree, the title it was gets your listing found, your photos are generally what sell the item. What the description does do is go into more detail about the item.

Try not to write a long essay like description, this can turn buyers off. Don't talk about yourself, keep it professional, not personal. (Obviously for used goods you can say comes from a smoke free home etc. but it's not advisable to go into detail about how you used to love camping and loved it so much you decided to upgrade to a caravan so your grandparents could travel with you, blah blah blah.)

Give details about the item features, the benefits (if applicable) and any issues if you are selling a used item.

An example of a good description would be:

(Brand Name) Slimming Pills

100% natural slimming pills containing ginseng and green tea, green tea is renowned for increasing metabolic rate, helping you burn fat- even while you sleep!

These pills contain no stimulants so will not cause palpitations or disrupted sleep like competing brands.

Free diet plan with every order, when ordered before 25th June!

* Note the call to action on the end which encourages the buyer to take action now!

11) Scroll down to the pricing structure. You will see two tabs; Auction and Fixed Price. Auction is where you start bidding at a price and buyers can bid on the item like they would at a live auction until it ends. At which

point the highest bidder wins the item. Then there is fixed price. Fixed price is where you choose a price you want for the items and buyer can simply buy it for that price- or submit a best offer if you choose to accept offers.

Auctions are often useful on used goods, however, when you have stock I would suggest using fixed price listings all the time for your items, so this is what I would like you to choose for this item. The reason you will use fixed price almost all of the time is fees. On a fixed price listing, you can have a listing selling 40 of the same item, for one listing fee. Whereas an auction is only for one item, so you would need 40 listings each charging you a fee. (You will also be charged a final value fee for every item you sell whether you used a fixed price listing or an auction style listing)

On top of this many buyers now prefer items they can buy immediately rather than waiting for an auction to end.

So, click the fixed price tab, add your buy it now price and click accept best offers if you wish to do so. Add your quantity and duration. For this item just try 5 or 7 days as these often get the best results. And leave the "start listing immediately box ticked"

12) Scroll down to how you will be paid and add your PayPal details and select any other payment methods you wish to accept.

13) Under postage you will select your chosen postage methods. As these change from country to country I cannot give you which

services to select. But I would suggest offering a free service wherever you can. Free shipping is proven to attract more buyers.

In future when you are more established you will want to offer at least one free and one express service. This is not only good customer service, but also EBay regard this highly and as part of the Top Rated Seller Program actually offer fee discounts for people who offer these at present. (EBay do change their programs and incentives regularly.) Becoming a top rated seller is something you want to aim for long term, although it can take a little while to achieve.

14) Dispatch time should be same or next working day.

15) Choose whether you want to offer international shipping yourself. If you do not offer international shipping on an item, EBay may enroll you into their global shipping program. This is where EBay charge your customer for shipping abroad and you ship to EBay's shipping depot, they then ship it abroad.

Offering international shipping is a good way to increase your sales, but you need to be careful what you try and ship abroad (some items cannot be shipped such as pressurized containers) and also what you charge for shipping abroad ad overseas delivery can be expensive and you could end up out of pocket.

16) For now you can ignore returns policy and additional information (when you upgrade to business seller you will need to follow the

steps to add a return policy but for now you don't need to worry about it) and simply click continue.

17) You will be asked to preview your listing and click submit on the next page.

18) Congratulations, your first item is for sale!

Chapter 3: What to Sell & Where to Get Them...

Ok, so you now have an account and have listed your first item or two for sale. You now need to decide what products you want to sell as a business.

On some platforms, such as <u>Amazon</u>, I would say choose one product and dominate the competition, however, with EBay the more products you have the more you seem to sell. This is probably because EBay is quite saturated with sellers now, as people seem to start selling on EBay before scaling up to add extra platforms.

Now as much as having 1000's of products and listings sounds great, in reality it's not practical. One, because I imagine most of you don't have a warehouse and staff just yet, two, because you probably don't have a few thousand to invest in stock and lastly, because when you first start selling on EBay you will only be allowed to have a limited number of items listed until you prove you are a competent seller, then you can gradually increase this limit.

So, what we do instead of this- at least for now; is find a niche. If you are interested in online business, you have probably heard this term many times in the past. A niche is a small section of the market in short. There are hundreds out there from weight loss to equestrian. Then you will begin to look at products within these niches and see if some brief research suggests it maybe a good option to sell.

1) Write down a list of 15 niches

2) For each of these 15 niches write down 5 product ideas

3) For each of these 5 product ideas narrow it down to three more micro niches

Example:

Niche:

Equestrian

5 Products in Equestrian Niche:

Riding Boots, Riding Hats, Horse Care Products, Tack, Books

Riding Boots Micro Niches:

Children's riding boots, long riding boots, jodhpur boots

Riding Hats Micro Niches:

Children's riding hats, Classic riding hats, Skull riding hats

Horse Care Products Micro Niches:

Horse shampoo, Horse fly spray, Horse grooming kit

Tack Micro Niches:

Saddles, Bridles, Stirrups

Books Micro Niches:

Horse care book, Horse breed book, Children's horse stories

The products you end up with don't necessarily have to make sense; the idea is that from this exercise you will have 15 niches, each with 20 product ideas for you to research. It is just a simple way of trying to come up with ideas that are not obvious ones.

So now you have a list of ideas it is time to do a little research as to whether these items will sell. To do this we will begin by looking at EBay completed listings.

1) Log into your <u>EBay</u> account

2) Type in the name of your product into the search box

3) On the left hand side scroll down to "show only" and select the box that says "completed listings"

What this does, is shows you all of the items on EBay that have already finished. The ones that are green sold. Count the listings on the first page; ideally you want 40- 50% of the listings in green. If more than half are green continue to the next step.

Look at the prices, the items you sell will be unbranded, so look at the first 10 unbranded listings that sold and write down how much they sold for and the postage charged.

Do this for a few products until you have a list of 5 or 6 different products that you have average pricing for.

This is the free way of finding out whether a niche will work or not. This method will give you a snapshot of what is selling over the last few days.

But there are also paid tools you can use that will analyze your niches success over a much longer period of time, and literally pull lots of information from EBay; Including the average selling price, average shipping cost, and the all-important sell through rate.

You can access a 7 day free trial of the tool here: EBay Tool

Now this tool, is excellent, it undertakes hours of research in minutes. However, because it analyses so many products. The sell through rate on here will be much lower than the small sample you have researched with completed listings. If you find a product that has an above 50% sell through rate you are onto a winner. However, any product over 30% is ok on here.

The tool itself is very self-explanatory, and when you find a product you would like more information on there are a couple more buttons for in depth stats that tell you which days your chosen product sells best on and what times. If you do choose to use this tool, make note of these as these will be the times you want your products to end.

Lastly, this tool has a "hot searches" section which automatically updates as consumers search for different items. Basically, it tells you which items are currently being searched for on EBay the most; which is an invaluable tool when choosing a new product to sell.

This tool also can analyze any of the EBay platforms for any country, so is useful if you decide to scale up outside of your own country at a later date and also Amazon.

I'm not going to spend too much time talking about the tool, as only some of you will decide to purchase it, and on top of that it really is very simple to use. But here is the link again in case you decide to give it a go, I really cannot recommend it enough. At the very least get your 7 day free trial so you can use it for your first product.

EBay Tool

One last thing to note on choosing a product (and something I have learnt the hard way) is to always choose a none-branded product. (at least 99% of the time) On some occasions you may be able to do a deal with the official distributor of a product, but most of the time, you won't be able to get enough discount to make a good profit. Never ever be tempted to order fake goods from China.

When you do your research on completed listings, only take prices for items that are none branded that you will be able to compete with.

Sourcing

So, now you have a list of possible products, let's think about sourcing them. Now any products you have on your list will be available somewhere, however, a business is not a business unless you can make a profit on that item.

You want to aim for at least a 40-50% profit margin (i.e. around half of the cost you sell the item for is profit.)

So take an average price including shipping (as we will always charge free shipping-EBay like this!) for the product you are searching for. Let's as an example say your item is a gel nail polish set that sells for $20 on average including shipping.

Out of $20 we would need to minus the cost of shipping this item, and a 10% EBay final value fee and the cost of the product. What is left is profit; ideally $8-10 dollars on a $20 item.

So on a small $20 item, final value fees will be about $2 (10%), Shipping at this point would be estimated, but let's for the sake of a small item it's $4.50 and we want to earn $8 minimum on a $20 item (around 40-50% of cost)

Add these up $2 + $4.50 + $8 = $14.50

Then subtract this from the price of the product $20 - $14.50 = $5.50

This means we need to source our product for $5.50 or less.

Now, this is just a guideline, if you are happy earning less than 40-50% profit margin, then you are free to add extra budget to your product sourcing.

So, where can we source products for this cheaply? Well in short, China.

There will be wholesalers and importers in your own country that will sell items very cheaply. But in my experience, the margins you get from China are much larger than those you would get in the UK.

Years ago, you had to buy a container full of products from China to get the huge discounts, but now anyone can access these discounts, even with small quantities.

In all honesty, sourcing the products is not the main battle; it's choosing what to sell that is the most important part of this whole process. However, being able to source the item cheaply is always a good thing to know.

Start by going to the link below

Wholesale Goods

This site is fantastic, manufacturers and wholesalers list on here the way we would list on EBay. The best thing about this site is that you can pay with your debit card (when you order from some of the larger cheaper manufacturers you usually pay via bank transfer) and it also has buyer protection, so if you do not receive your item you are guaranteed your money back.

These are not the cheapest prices ever, but I have bought many items on here I have sold for a large profit. Sterling silver jewelry is a prime example. I have purchased sterling silver necklaces on this site for 66c including shipping on this site and sold them on for

$9.99.

The great thing about this site is you can start your business for next to no outlay, because, there are no large minimum orders- and most of the sellers offer larger discounts for bulk orders.

If you do happen to have a bit more capital to start your EBay business it's worth looking at this site's sister site : <u>Bulk Wholesale Products</u>

 this site is mainly manufacturers, requiring larger orders. However, the prices are MUCH cheaper and sometimes you can ask for a sample order of a smaller quantity if you contact the suppliers on here.

The downside of this site is that there is no buyer protection and you usually have to pay via bank transfer. So if you order from here you do so at your own risk. I have had many good experiences on this site, and only one or two bad. If you are going to order on this site I would suggest ordering a small sample order to check out the supplier's legitimacy before placing a larger order. This is also a good idea as you want to see the quality of the goods you are buying.

When you contact suppliers on <u>Alibaba</u> you need to message them and ask them for prices and MOQ (minimum order quantities) and always contact a few suppliers on here as some may not get back to you.

Remember, if you're ordering for business purposes you may be charged import taxes when the goods arrive in your country. These taxes vary from country to country.

In my experience, if you're ordering a small order (for example when I first started I used to order 50pcs of one necklace) the order can sometimes slip through the tax system unnoticed if being sent by standard air mail, however, they sometimes get charged when being sent via courier.

This is just something to think about when deciding on a quantity to order. It is not guaranteed as even a small order can be charged this, and not all countries will have this tax. But I want you to be aware of everything from the start.

Don't forget- Prices are usually negotiable! Even on **Aliexpress**, if you come to place a second order, contact the supplier first and ask for a discount. Remember to tell them you want to create a long term business relationship with them.

Also, you can also try and locate suppliers in your own country. You may well struggle to get the kinds of prices you would on these sites, but sometimes, it is much simpler to be able to contact a supplier over the phone and have next day shipping so it's always worth a try.

You can also try drop shipping. This is where some suppliers offer a service where they will send a product direct to your customer. The margins are usually much smaller, but effectively, you have nothing to do but list the item and send an email to the supplier. They usually deal with problems if an item goes astray and deal with shipping etc. and you have no stock to hold. Another benefit of this is you'll never be left with stock. You only pay for what you need.

If you have a spare room or garage, I would always suggest going for the higher margins and holding small amounts of stock. Although I usually have a few suppliers (wholesale from China and locally and dropship) selling various items so that I have multiple income streams.

You can search around Google for dropshippers or wholesalers based in your country by typing "Dropshippers (YOUR COUNTRY)" or "(PRODUCT) Wholesaler"

Although I mainly purchase from China, I have included a site which has vetted suppliers all over the world who also dropship (This site is a paid site, but is well worth the subscription as it saves a lot of time tracking down the suppliers yourself.)

World Brands A directory of high quality dropshippers and wholesalers. All of the companies listed on here are vetted.

Chapter 4: Making EBay Easier...

Giving a Professional Image

So, now you have your first items on the way, you want to start and think about giving your account a professional image ready for when you list your first item.

Now all of these are just suggestions, however, appearing more business-like will entice more customers.

The first thing you need to consider is upgrading to a business account. I suggest you all do this as quickly as possible. Yes it makes it official; you are a business rather than someone selling their old belongings. But buyers look upon this favorably when buying items.

So to do this go to My EBay, click account and under personal information click edit next to where is says "personal account". It will then walk you through some steps asking for business information etc.

Once you are registered as a business seller you want to think about whether you would like to invest in a shop. Now, as a seller you get a number of free listings every month, if you open a shop, you get extra of these free listings. So at some point when you have more products, I would suggest opening a shop. For now, if you only have one or two items then it's ok to just be a business seller.

There are of course other benefits of having an EBay shop such as reduced listing fees outside your free listings. You really should weigh up the pros and cons of being a shop for you personally. You can do this by going to My EBay, Subscriptions and under shops there is a section that says "learn more" which will give you all of the benefits of being a shop. Weigh up whether this is worthwhile for you and your business at present, and remember, you can upgrade to a shop at any time.

If you do choose to upgrade to a shop, you will want to get a shop theme designed to give a much more professional look. You can get these designed cheaply by searching EBay. You will also want a listing template, whether you open a shop or not. Many sellers offer a shop and listing theme package for quite cheaply.

The designer usually installs the shop theme. Listing templates are designed and given to you in the form of code (Which you would insert into the HTML box when you enter the description at the time of creating a listing.)

Listing Your Inventory

Now this section is particularly important. These are tips I have learnt with time and experience.

We have touched upon the importance of the title, but what I like to do is ensure that regardless which search tool the buyer's use, that one of my listings will appear on the first search page. This can mean that you have 2-3 listings for each product (hence the reason those shop's come in handy)

When someone searches on EBay, the results are automatically shown as "best match" results; this is based on keywords as discussed in the initial chapter.

There are a few options that the buyer can choose but in my experience, they will either leave it at best match or select "ending soonest" or "lowest price plus shipping"

For best match, there is not a lot we can do about this as it's based on keywords and how established our account and our listing is, you will find your listings will rank better the longer they have been active. This is why the first listing you create after you become a business seller will not be for a 3 or 5 day listing, it will be on the "good 'til cancelled" This is a buy it now listing where you will list a large amount of products and it will stay on EBay until those products have sold. (I tend to look at the quantity left in your active listings weekly and update the good til cancelled listings to a higher quantity if they are getting low so they remain on permanently.

These are the listings that will in time appear in the best match search.

If a buyer selects ending soonest, your good 'til cancelled listings will be nowhere near the top of the search, so you will need to create a second listing for the product that is only 3 days long. So it always appears near the top of the ending soonest listings as well. (We will talk about how to automatically get these to relist in the next section so you do not have to constantly track these items.)

Lastly, for the lowest price plus shipping search. If you're item price is lower than most of your competitors you should appear near the top for this search so you do not have to worry about it. However, if you are not (and sometimes you do not have to be the cheapest to make a lot of sales- you'll need to test various price points) you will need to create a listing variation.

Listing variations are not available to personal sellers so you cannot use this technique unless you're registered as a business seller.

When you are going through the seller form, you will come to a section that says list multiple variations of your item. EBay have a great page with instructions in the help section if you're struggling with this, but the form is quite simple to follow. What you will want to do is add a "trial" or "small" version of your item for a very cheap price.

For example, when selling slimming pills, we offered a 3 pill trial pack for 99c. This means when the buyer changes the search to "lowest price plus shipping" we will appear there.

I have seen people who sell envelopes offer one envelope, or people who sell phone covers offer a plastic screen protector.

Now, this means you could have 2 or 3 listings for each item. EBay do not like duplicate listings, and if they look the same they will remove them. So what you need to do is change the titles around. Re-arrange the wording, add or remove some keywords, make them different enough that EBay's automated system will not pick them up as duplicates.

These are tips I learnt only from time and experience, and you will find very few people willing to tell a newbie these tips as they don't want their businesses spoilt. However, the way I look at it is there are plenty of niches to go around!

Lastly, if you have a lot of products to list, you can list a lot of them in bulk by using EBay's free tool Turbo Lister (Google Turbo Lister and you will be given the most recent link to the download page) I personally do not use Turbo Lister, because I have managed to automate most of my listings (which I will discuss in the next section) however, it is a very good tool and worth checking out to see if it will help you personally.

Automation

My favorite part! This is the part where you can automate all of the hard parts so you can concentrate on your sales and customer service!

Under My EBay > subscriptions you will see a product called Seller Manager Pro. Seller manager Pro has a very small monthly subscription cost and will automate so much of your process.

When you subscribe, you will log into My EBay and see a section for Seller Manager Pro which has an option for automation preferences. In here you want to go in and set it to leave positive feedback whenever a buyer leaves one for you.

You can also automate it to send your buyer emails whenever an item is marked shipped etc.

This in itself saves mountains of time- especially when you get up to making lots of sales every day but that's not all.

When you view on your active items under selling, you will now see a button at the top that says automation rules. You can check the box next to the products on three day auctions, select the automation rules and assign a rule for the product to automatically relist when it ends. Brilliant! This means once your item is up, you don't have to maintain it unless the item changes! (Other than adding quantity onto your good 'til cancelled listings)

I should state though until you've been selling a while, the amount of items you can list will be restricted. (You will be able to request a higher limit every 6 weeks- make sure you do this!) This does however mean that an automation rule can fail if you do not have enough listings left for the month. Just something to think about when you assign the rules. Long term though, this tool is invaluable to your business.

Another thing I like to do (which is optional) is to collate a mailing list of all the buyers PayPal addresses, so I can email them offers of products in the future. Now let me stress, your buyers must be aware they are being added to a mailing list. So what I do is I offer them something free and tell them about it in the listing.

For example,

Buy these slimming pills today, and receive a diet plan delivered free of charge direct to your inbox! (Please note in order to receive this free item you will be added to our priority customer mailing list. If you do not want to receive further information and offers from us then you can just click unsubscribe in the email once your plan has been delivered)

So you will need to create something free, for example, if you're selling craft items, you may offer a guide to card making. Just something you can quickly create in word, or outsource on somewhere like www.fiverr.com

So you will need somewhere to put these emails, if you want to do it free and use your time to do this task, you can do so by manually entering your customers PayPal addresses into a spreadsheet, and importing them to your email whenever you want to send them out an email.

However, I prefer to automate this process and I do so using two tools.

The first is an email auto responder. It will collect and store your customer's emails, and you can set up an automated newsletter to be delivered when a buyer subscribes to automatically send out their free gift.

Here is a link to my preferred choice of auto

responder, because they simply have incredible email newsletter templates that look so professional and it's very simple to use, it even tells you how many people opened your email correspondence.

http://bit.ly/1SzbftE

This means when you have built up a list of subscribers you can email them with an offer when you launch a new product, or even give them a discount on your current product range.

You will need to request single opt in by emailing their customer service team, this means the buyer won't have to click subscribe in an email as well before their item is delivered, but if you explain to them it's to deliver a free gift to your customer and they have agreed to it, they will allow this.

So this automates the sending out of the free gift once they are on your mailing list, but you can also automate the process of getting them onto your mailing list. So they are automatically added when they purchase something on EBay.

This link below is an incredible tool, in which you will link your PayPal address and your auto responder account. When a sale is made, the tool pulls the details from the buyers PayPal, and adds them as a contact on your auto responder.

Here is the link for this tool:

http://bit.ly/1Jfl1j5

Both of these are paid tools, building a mailing list is a fantastic way of creating extra sales and therefore profits. You can also create buttons within your PayPal account (under profile) which will allow you to make sales directly from the emails you send out rather than through EBay meaning you're saving the EBay fees.

Chapter 5: Building the Business

Achievement within EBay

We have already spoken about the importance of Feedback and Detailed Seller Ratings within EBay, but these are some of the contributing factors to achieving higher statuses such as Powerseller and Top Rated Seller.

EBay's Powerseller programme has been running for many years, and although it does not have direct benefits from EBay, customers look highly upon Powerseller status.

EBay's sales dashboard will keep you up to date with how far you are off achieving each Powerseller level.

By becoming a Powerseller your sales should increase because customers will trust you as a provider more. But the goal you really want to aim for is EBay's Top Rated Seller. You can achieve Top Rated Seller status at any of the Powerseller levels.

It can be quite difficult to maintain as it means your detailed seller ratings have to have less than 2% under 3 stars, but if you have a product that delivers what you say it shouldn't be too far from achievable and maintainable. Just ensure you don't over promise in your descriptions.

If you gain Top Rated Seller status, your

listings get more visibility- a massive advantage in EBay selling. You also get 15% off final value fees on qualifying listings. (Criteria for qualifying listings changes now and again but can be found on EBay's site, but includes things like offering an express and a free delivery option on listings. I would suggest doing this from the start as it's a good practice.)

Increasing Margins

Increasing margins is one of the biggest things I can advise you to do. Many sellers get their listings up and they are selling from them, so they just leave them.

There is always more profit to squeeze from each item. Here are some examples.

PayPal: PayPal offer a discount on their fees for sellers selling over a certain amount. This is very little known knowledge, as you have to email customer services to ask about it.

Postage: Many couriers or postal services offer discounts for bulk and their prices are almost always negotiable. Do this regularly as your business grows. Most standard post services have a business option where you can save on regular postage fees.

Packing Materials: When you can afford to ask for bulk pricing on items, as buying in bulk will get you cheaper deals. You can also consider buying packing from China even cheaper.

Products: Again, negotiate with your supplier, order a slightly larger quantity each time for a bigger discount.

All of these little things help! Don't let your profit margins go stale!

Scaling Up

Once you've mastered EBay and feel you've learned all you can and added more ranges, there are so many other avenues you can scale up to.

Firstly, EBay has a separate site for almost every country, it's worth looking into these to see if it's worth listing separately on each site.

Secondly, there are other sites around similar to EBay such as Etsy (which sells mainly craft products)

Amazon is one of the major e-commerce players. I would strongly suggest scaling up to Amazon after EBay.

You could also consider building your own website. This does not have to be as complicated as it sounds. Many website builders now are cheap and some have built in marketing tools.

Here are a couple you could use:

This site offers free and paid options to create a nice website, and it's very simple with their click and drop system.

Website Builder Simple

This site offers a premium looking site for low cost. It also has integrated marketing tools to help you sell more products. Great value for money and very simple to use.

Website Builder

Chapter Six: Building Your Online Brand and Business Beyond eBay

When you have your own business you're put into a unique position of creating a new world around you. Not only do you get to create your own brand but you also create experiences for customers, you get to create the world around them – even if you don't have a physical store front. Your Ebay page, website, and even the smallest details like the online shopping cart will help immerse your customers into your world. I want to tackle all of those topics in this chapter. Let's start with the biggest topic first: your brand.

Guide to Your Online Brand:

First you have to determine what your brand is.

It's more than just what your logo is, what your products look like, and what type of merchandizing you use. It is all about the overall experience that your customers have when using and enjoying your business. Of course, that means that it covers a majority of factors including (but not limited to) what types of practices you and your team members have, how you go about your business, what the customer service and interactions are like, how you share information with them, your marketing plans, social media interactions, your visual cues and elements (tags, labels, etc.), and how your customers interact with your products.

It is essential to consider as many senses as possible when looking at your brand. A good example out be of one of the teen brands in our local mall. You can smell that store as soon as you come within fifty feet of the front door. Is that good branding or bad branding? Well, the scent wouldn't be overall unpleasant if it wasn't so strong. Because of this, there are always a few negative murmurs as others walk by the store.

The marketing aspect of that decision is can be considered successful. After all, that scent is now synonymous with their brand – every time we get a whiff of that cologne or perfume, we think of the store. In addition to that, we know the company's name because of it. However, for most of us, it holds a negative connotation or correlation now.

You might be thinking, "Well, that doesn't apply to me. I don't have a storefront." While that may be true, think of it this way: when you ship your products, the scent that comes from the box and its contents will remain until the customer opens it. What type of scent will come from the contents of that parcel? I have seen a number of packages that come from overseas, which smell of fish and other unpleasant scents. If you know that the materials you use will have a strong odor of plastic (or something more unpleasant), consider airing out your materials before you box it up. Another option would be to warn your customers of the odor in an email and suggest that they air out their products for a day or wash the product first. There will be more about shipping later in this chapter.

What about visual cues? What colors stand out? Remember that standing out means that you have to be different. While "being different" is not just restricted to visual cues like color, you must keep this concept in mind when you think about the aesthetic aspect of your brand. What colors do you want associated with your brand? Do you want something strong and powerful in order to stand out next to the other brands in your niche? Or would something soft and subtle appeal to more of your target market? Consider also: font use and formatting, shapes, images, and the use of the background color.

Now let's go deeper and talk about the best marketing tool at your disposal: word of mouth. No matter what your platform is, your best lead generator will always be word of mouth. If you have quality products, your customers will tell their friends, family, acquaintances, and complete strangers about it. You can be as charming as the most charismatic of businesswomen and businessmen but if you don't have the products and services to back it up, your customers won't return.

In addition to that, you have to keep away from complacency. It is "easy" to develop a product which your customers enjoy, then mass produce it. However, you have to keep evolving. Refine it. Test new options and offer new ideas and alternatives. If you end up with tunnel vision for your business, make sure that it is on the evolution and improvement of your product, not on the money that you can and will bring in.

Don't forget "you" in your brand!

Believe it or not, one of the main reasons why a number of small businesses fail is due to the lack of appearances made by the owner. Yes, you are a part of your brand. You need to make sure that you are visible and you are being proactive. You can't let your business just run itself. Not only is that lazy, it is also ineffective. Your customers need to know who you are and that you are the fact of your business. How do you do this?

First of all, you need to fill out the Ebay profile in a friendly, yet professional way. Use a conversational tone when you describe your products, in order to show off your voice and personality. When you talk about the different aspects of your business, make sure that you are showing off the passion that you have for your business or product. Your clients and customers should be able to feel your energy when you "speak" through your profile, descriptions, summaries, and through your other marketing materials. If a customer feels like they 'know you' they are more likely to purchase again from you. Don't just focus on trying to convert browsers to buyers, it's just as important to focus on converting customers to repeat customers.

Now, some of these things will come naturally by using your EBay profile etc, but there are also other things you can do to help this process along. One is by using other methods to promote your products. These can include

Facebook, Twitter and other social media, and even as you grow your own website.

Time and time again I have seen people make money selling a product that they have created a video review or tutorial with on YouTube, take the time to do these things. They can be recorded with a click of a button on your phone and you can include links to the EBay products in the description. Easy extra traffic!

Social media is a very powerful form of marketing today, and you should utilize this free method in any way you can to drive traffic to your EBay page and as you grow your website etc. You should be making a presence on other social media sites and on your own website.

Your website should be an extension of you and your brand. The way that it is set up, the colors that you use, the formatting and style of fonts, the images of your products, and the other things that you offer, should showcase your personality, your passion, and your energy, but more than that, provide a consistency across all of your platforms. So use the same logo and color scheme on your EBay as you do on your Google plus , Facebook, Youtube and Website, use the same photograph of yourself if you are building a brand around you as a person. It make your business more recognizable to customers and gives you a more professional appearance.

Remember, not to be overwhelmed by adding all of these extra traffic sources. You will find many of them will come with natural progression as your business develops, and they are a great way to scale your business, however, I have known many people have huge businesses on EBay alone, without any need for additional marketing. These things are meant to compliment your EBay activity, not replace it.

You might be worried that you only have a limited number of products and could not fill out a website, well don't worry. A website is about your brand not your products. So what else can you offer on your site? Business websites (especially small online businesses) should offer at least two of these three things: products to sell to customers, information for their customers, and/or entertainment for your customers. The key is that these things should be, "for your customers". They need to be able to get something out of your website. This will keep them coming back for more. So for example, if you sell knitting equipment, on your website you might have knitting patters which are free, you can then either direct visitors to your EBay store to buy knitting products, or you can sell directly to them on your website.

Information for Your Customers

Offering information on your website can help gain continued views on your website. In order to utilize this platform well, make sure that the information you provide your customers (tutorials, for example) uses items from your eBay and make sure that you also add the links to your eBay listings at the end of the informative articles, blog posts, videos, or podcasts.

What kind of information should you offer your visitors?

Let's look at ideas you could create free information about to attract traffic to your website and in turn to your products. Let's say that you are selling homemade quilts on eBay. There are many different types of information that you can offer your visitors.

- Tips on how to make their own quilts at home,
- Information about different quilts that are available on your eBay site,
- Tips on how to take care of the quilts that they buy from you,
- A funny informative history of quilts,
- Tips on how to decorate your home with quilts,
- Advice on different types of quilts,
- Information about mending quilts,
- Etc.

You can just as easily write or talk about information for your collection or refurbished items that you sell on eBay. Some examples would be:

- Appropriate maintenance on vintage items,

- Tips on quick appraisals while shopping online or in antique stores,

- Historical information about your vintage products,

- Tips on how to reupholster or refurbish items,

- Suggested alternative uses for vintage items,

- Advice on how to decorate a home with antique products,

Remember to always use different types of media in order to catch as many different views as possible. Articles, videos, and podcasts are the three main ways to convey information.

In addition to informative pieces, consider putting up a blog on your site. This is a great way for visitors to find information about you and your eBay site. You will be able to show the viewers the person behind the business. Making your company more personable to your customer base is a great way to connect with them.

Utilizing the Online Space:

If you want to take your eBay seller profile and turn it into a large business, you will look at scaling to a website at some point. It makes sense to do this as it is one of the natural progression steps. As with any business, there are some start up costs invol

How much will it cost (in start- up fees) to start a business online?

This is usually the first question asked when talking about starting a new business (no matter what kind of business it is), so let's break it down.

1. Webhosting. A decent webhosting cost is anywhere between ten dollars to about twenty dollars per month. There are a few different options and – depending on how tech savvy you are and how much you need in terms of help – but many companies have special offers on that you can take advantage of when you come to set up your site.

2. Email Marketing – Email services that will help you with marketing are great and they generally run about twenty dollars a month. An email list will be one of your best options when it comes to making money online. When you're focusing on eBay, it might not seem like an essential but it is. So don't skip this step. There are two steps to this particular start-up figure: setting up and gathering your email list and choosing the service provider that will work best in your situation. Depending on what you do, what products you provide, and the set-up of your

business, some email marketing services might work better for you than others. My favorite is Get Response as they have readymade templates for you to email out to your customers. You can join get response by visiting here: http://www.getresponse.com/index/staceycdc

3. Processors for Your Incoming Payments. There isn't normally an upfront cost for this particular step of your start-up. Most people use PayPal because it is easy and pretty universal, but there are other options While there might not be an upfront fee for all of these, there is usually a fee per transaction. Depending on the company, that could run anywhere from four to twelve percent of each transaction.

4. A Shopping Cart Application or Program. These generally cost anywhere from around five dollars a month to $30 a month. Some payment processors come with shopping carts so a separate application won't be needed.

5. Web Design. This cost varies depending on what you do. The cost for a premade design can be fairly inexpensive but you do run the risk of looking like a handful of other company websites. Many companies now offer drag and drop websites builders which are ideal.

Recommendations for new website

owners is to go simple. Fancy designs are great but if you really want to build a following, you need a website that visitors and users can easily navigate.

You can easily get off the ground with a $100 price tag if you know exactly what you want and if you have all of your basics set up before you dive in head first.

Organizing and Writing Information For Your Site

You might not be able to put informative articles on your website on a regular basis because of other life factors or because these types of articles, videos, or podcasts take a while to produce. Remember that when you post something on your site, the goal of the article, blog post, video, or podcast should be one of three things:

- To inform the reader about something
- To entertain the reader
- To inspire the reader

If you don't have the material to inform the reader about something this week, why not post a funny quip, story, or anecdote? If you don't have anything along those lines, try to inspire your visitor with something: a quote, a picture, an image of your new product line-up, or an inspirational story.

Shipping Your Brand:

Shipping is an incredibly important part of your eBay transaction because it is a great way for you to communicate with your customers in order to guarantee their satisfaction and continued business.

In this section we will talk about

- A few ways you can save money on shipping,
- The perks of offering free shipping, and
- How to personalize the package for your customers

Tip**Many courier companies offer discounted rates to EBay sellers! Go onto some of their websites and find the best offers local to you.

FedEx loves eBay sellers (probably due to how much business they can get from them). They have volume discount rates for sellers that can save you up to 37% on various services.

USPS Offers Discounts for eBay Sellers who have the Right Qualifications.

Any eBay top-rated sellers and sellers that have an average of around 2500 transactions or more each month can get something called Commercial Plus Pricing. This is an offer that will save you up to 35% on your Priority Mail (domestic) and Priority Mail Express packages. You don't even have to enroll in anything elaborate. If you're a qualified, you automatically receive the savings when you print and pay for your postage.

UPS has Discounts as Well.

UPS has a special pricing program for eBay sellers which gives you different types of discounts depending on what standard rates.

You Can Get Free Things Too!

Did you know that you can order free shipping supplies from the USPS? This includes flat rate boxes, shipping supplies, and regional rate boxes. Check out this link for more details: http://ebaysupplies.usps.com/usps.

In addition, if you go to UPS.com, you can get air shipping packaging, self-adhesive labels, and other packaging supplies free from UPS.

Consider Offering Free Shipping

When customers and online buyers are looking at one of your products, they see the total cost before deciding on which item to buy. The price of your actual product may be low but if shipping costs even more than the product, it will hike up the whole price in your customers' minds. People love the concept of free shipping. In fact, there are buyers out there who only search for items that have free shipping. Others consider this a deal breaker when they have to choose between two different items. Because of this, free shipping will even pay for itself due to the number of customers that it can attract.

When considering whether or not to offer free shipping, remember these benefits:

- You will catch the eye of more shoppers,

- The Final Value Fees will be lower when it is applied to the full amount of the sale. This includes shipping.

- It will boost your search results when it comes to listings with a fixed price.

- It will generate an automatic five-star rating (on your shipping) when the buyer selects "free shipping".

Personalizing Your Packaging

You can personalize your packaging in different ways. Most amateur eBay sellers don't spend the time to use this as a way to heighten their customers' experience or use it as a way to reach out to them. There are a number of ways to use packaging in a special way.

Package inserts. are a great way to increase your revenue and customer loyalty – if you do it right. Package inserts are great because:

- Inserts are perfect for selling products that are similar to what the customer just ordered.

- Inserts are low cost.

- Inserts are great for moving merchandise that you need to liquidate.

- Personalizing them makes the customer feel important, special, and cared for.

- You have already paid for the package! Consider it as free advertising.

There are five different types of inserts that you can put into the packages of the orders that you ship.

1. Personal notes and thank you cards. This is definitely the most personalized type of interaction you can get with your customers – short of talking with each of them one-on-one. A simple thank you card can be incredibly powerful because it is a thoughtful gesture. We were all taught to say "thank you" and write thank you notes when we were young. Being reminded of this when we are older is a great way to bring back those lessons of respect and gratitude that we learned when we were kids. Plus, this is a great way to "one up" large corporations since they

can't personalize thank you cards like small businesses can.

2. Thank you gifts. You don't have to buy them a new car or expensive items. A small package of candy, some mints, removable tattoos, a baseball card, or mini brochures, are great options. Package them in a little branded Ziploc bag. Remember that this is also an extension of your brand so consider the item carefully. You wouldn't send a baseball card as a gift for someone who just ordered a cardigan sweater or a leather briefcase. Your gift says something about you and your company as well. Match it to your brand and match it to your clients.

3. Product samples. If you are able to add product samples to your packages, it is a great way to cross sell your products to different customers. Introducing your customers to different product lines is a wonderful way to boost your revenue and..., who doesn't love samples? It is a great surprise for your patrons.

4. Customization stickers and decals. This is a great way to hype up your business and brand name. It is also a great way for your customers to customize their products for as long as they want.

5. Survey, product review request, or a share request on social media. For a lot of customers, this signifies the end of the transaction. They bought an item

and now they are receiving it. Since it is the "end", ask them to share their experience with other people. In addition, don't forget to ask them if you can improve on the service in any way.

6. Discounts. This is the most popular type of product insert. While you can just as easily send these out in a mass email (those email lists are a great way to market), it is just as important to send them out as inserts as well. Consider printing them out in business card sizes so your customers can slip them into their wallets. Whenever they go through their wallets, they will be reminded of your company. Also consider slipping in two different discount offers: one for your customer and one for that customer to hand out. Word of mouth is a great advertising tool after all.

   This is also a great way to test out which types of offers your customers respond to the most:

   - Free _____ on the next item you order
   - $___ credit toward the next item you order
   - ___% off of the next item you order
   - BOGOF items (specific details apply)

   Play with the wording and play with

the different types of offers that you send out to see which type(s) get the most responses.

Package inserts are all about going one step further and matching the product and the customer with the right types of offering. It is a direct marketing technique after all, so it should be personalized and should be used to increase sales, profit, and loyalty.

The packaging is just as important as what is inside. When you receive a box from a company, certain feelings and emotions well up inside. When customers receive a box with the Amazon logo scrawled on the outside of the cardboard, they feel ecstatic. Sure, it is exciting to receive any box. However, if you can incite that extra excitement – the excitement that customers feel when an Amazon box arrives on their doorstep – you'll be able to give your customer a better experience.

The outside packaging is important. Are you going to use a regular, brown cardboard box? Are you going to put your logo on the front in bold lettering? (Which can be another form of advertising.) Are you going to use a specific color? Is it going to be a cardboard box? Are you going to use recycled material?

The same questions can be asked about the types of packaging you use inside the box. Are they going to be a specific color? Recycled material, yes or no? Styrofoam popcorn? Shredded paper? Tissue paper? What do you

Engage as many senses as possible while you are packing the box. Remember that wherever you package the box, lingering odors may be present and will waft from the contents when your customer opens it. Do you have pets? Make sure not to package your items around your pets where a stray hair, feather, or other un-pleasantries can find their way inside the box.

Lately, a plethora of shipments from companies like Amazon have had additions of chocolate mints, hard candies, or other types of sweets in their boxes as a small gift. This is a great way to engage another sense for your customers.

Chapter Seven: Avoiding Common Online Business Mistakes

These tips work for anyone who intends on selling their products on eBay or if they want to venture out and start selling on other platforms or on their own website.

Jump in the Deep End. A mistake I have seen many entrepreneurs make is start with the Facebook Page, and the Youtube Channel, and try and build an audience on there before listing a single product for sale. While it is smart to try and build an audience to market to whenever you launch a new product, don't put off your main business activity to do this! LIST YOUR PRODUCT FIRST, if you wait for too long, you could easily get stuck on the idea of building an audience for months before you actually offer up anything for that audience. If you haven't yet started this process, you may be thinking to yourself, *why would you wait to launch?* There are many reasons for this, including:

- Waiting to gain a certain number of followers, subscribers, or visitors: 100, 1,000, 10,000, etc.

- Focusing so much on gaining an audience that they can't work on perfecting or building the product in the first place,

- Using this "platform building" or "audience building" as an excuse to *NOT* create a product. Unfortunately, some people destroy their chances of success before they even start. This could be due to a fear of failure or even a fear of success. They could be afraid that no one will actually want to buy it. Perhaps they don't want to put in all that work, only to have it ill received.

The great thing about EBay is it is a readymade platform with readymade buyers. You do not need to go out and get a website or a Facebook page, it is wise to do so in the long run, but if you want to start your business in the most simple way possible, just start listing your items for sale!

If you're worried about selling a quality product, consider running a couple beta tests with a group of people who will be honest with you. This will not only give you answers about your product but will also help you when it comes to learning about customer service. Listening to your customers is the best way to build on your business and make sure that you've got a quality product. Great customer service and word of mouth are the best forms of marketing.

Make sure you're focusing on a good niche. If you want to make sure that your product is wanted, ensure that it solves a problem for your customers. If you solve a problem that is significant enough, your customers will find you. You can also look at this from the opposite direction. If you want to find your niche, think about who would benefit most from this problem- solving product.

More often than not, businesses fail because they are trying to solve a problem that no one is concerned about. If you put your product out there and have no takers, you might need to look for a different problem to solve instead of a bigger audience.

Being different is the key to standing out amongst the competition. There are very few people who will find no competition for what they are selling on EBay. You will always have competition and that isn't necessarily a bad thing. Competition is great for businesses because it forces them to grow and develop better products. It forces businessmen to be more innovative and creative. A healthy sense of competition forces us to think in different ways – challenging our desire to be complacent and lazy. It also shows that other people are making money from your product or niche, so it means that it is more profitable.

Customers have multiple options to choose from in every market they shop for. When they look for shoes, they are bombarded with advertisements, colors, and styles. When they finally decide on one or two brands, they still have to go through fittings and comfort testing. This happens in every market to different degrees.

Coming out with a quality product will trump most other categories but you still need to stand out a bit. If you don't have a good eBay product listing (one that catches the eye) or if you don't have something about your product or marketing techniques that make you unique, you will be shadowed by other brands. You may have a quality product but if you can't get the attention of customers, it will take a while for them to find you.

Price is one way to stand out, but sometimes perceived value can cause issues, for example, if you have a product and you are cheaper than all other sellers, potential customers may think it's because your product is lower quality. When it comes to balance you need to decide who you are targeting your product at.

There are also other ways to stand out, free gifts, free shipping and being able to collect in person are all things potential customers could look for. Really think about ways you can stand out from your competition. What do you look for when shopping on EBay?

Don't be afraid of showing off your passion for your work if you are selling a product you make. If you're creating something new or if you are collecting/refurbishing items for resale, you should be working with something that you love, right? Passion is one of those contagious emotions. If you are passionate about your work, that enthusiasm and excitement will flow through your items and will come through your mannerisms and phrasing. Other people will catch on.

Do you have the right frame of mind?
You have to have a positive, yet realistic mindset in order to achieve your goals in business. Being in the right state of mind is more important than you think. Scientists and researchers are consistently publishing studies about the power or optimism and the negatively impactful pessimistic state of mind. If you believe you can achieve something, you are more likely to do it, many business people do not put enough emphasis on the power of having a good mindset, however, I have now met and worked with many successful entrepreneurs, who all have one thing in common, positive mindset. Many of them utilize tools such as goal setting and mapping every day in order to ensure they are on the right path to success.

Are you expecting success to happen quickly? Each stage of the process comes with different goals and different time frames. The very beginning will be the toughest. You have to build your clientele from scratch and start with a blank sheet of paper. The key is to (1) not expect success overnight and (2) be patient and don't get disappointed too easily. If you find that one marketing technique isn't working, work on a different idea. Remember that wallowing in any failure won't help push you forward. Don't give up at the first hurdle, we all experience them, it's the ones of us who continue to strive beyond these failures that make money.

Are you spending more time thinking about getting your business off of the ground and rather than *doing* things to get it off of the ground? Daydreaming about your business, thinking of possibilities, and brainstorming ideas are great ways to get started but don't use them as an excuse to procrastinate about the launch of your eBay listings, website, or to go full steam ahead into your business.

Do you have a partner in crime? Are you going at this all by yourself? There is no need for you to go into an eBay business by yourself. You may be thinking of profits ("Why divide the profits in half when you can keep it all for yourself?") but this of it this way: If you double your efforts, you'll double – or even triple – your profits. The more profits, the more you can split. As an added bonus, each person brings a different expertise to the business. You may be the brains behind the outfit and you may know how to refurbish, collect, or make the products. However, your new partner might be better at marketing, creating product listings, or setting up and maintaining the website. Focus on your skillset, can you do all of the things you need to do, or will you need to outsource some of them. Are you planning on keeping your job for a while, if so will you need someone to help share some of the work in the beginning? Luckily, this business model in particular is very flexible, and this means that you can mould it to be what you need it to be, but don't make it difficult for your business to grow just because you didn't have enough time to put into it, if this is the case, consider whether the possibility of going into business with a partner is viable for you.

Make sure that you have a brand. Actually, everyone has a brand. The difference is to have a distinctive brand that you purposefully put out to the public. A company name, a swanky logo, and some unique marketing materials is just the beginning of a brand. Branding is about how everyone sees you and your company. Yes, especially YOU. From your customer service skills, the wording in the eBay listings, your "about" page, to the special "thank you" that you send out – all of these things have to do with branding because they all influence how the public perceives you.

Are you overlooking every day maintenance? All businesses need to consider 'the boring stuff' like accounts, backing up data, keeping data etc. You need to ensure you comply with all laws and guidelines, so by this I mean, are you holding customer information appropriately with data protection in mind? Are all of your tax declarations up to date?

If your PC broke down tomorrow and you lost all of your product images and descriptions, do you have backups? Would you be able to get your listings back into place quickly or would you b frantically searching through files and folders looking for them? These things sound like mundane tasks to worry about at a later date, but I have learned over time that systems are important in the general running of a business and can save you time and money in the long run.

I back up my PC at the end of every week, and believe it or not, I have had to call on this back up numerous times!

Another important part of maintenance is your actual listings themselves, try not to let them go stale! Change the 'feel' of them using images and fonts etc sporadically. For example, many people add 'Christmas' graphics to their listings around the holiday season.

Have you chosen a way to measure your progress? Business, like any other worthy venture, is a learning process. You will be learning as you go along. You have to be able to measure your progress, learn from your mistakes, and focus on the big picture. Setting up an eBay page and posting a few listings isn't going to guarantee profits for you, and this is a mistake I see time and time again. People look at a product and see it's $5 and sells for $15 and think 'great I am making $10!" but they don't budget for the EBay fees, the Paypal fees, shipping from the supplier to you, shipping from you to the customer, packaging materials, stationary, marketing, it all adds up.

It's important that you track all of your

business ins and outs so you can see which products are profitable and which are not. Not all will be!

There are many software packages on the market that will help you to do this, however, a basic spreadsheet is quite enough. You should review this regularly, after a month, have you made more or less sales than you initially planned? How can you improve this? Are there any products you need to drop?

Look at the bigger picture as well, where do you want to be year from now? How much would you need to be making each month to get there? Are you no track to do this? Make goals for yourself when it comes to your business. Set benchmarks for yourself. Just make sure that those goals are SMART:

- Specific. Get as specific as you can. Don't just say that you want to sell X number of products. Break it down. For example, let's say that you knit items for sale. A specific goal wouldn't be "I want to sell 15 items this month." A specific goal would be, "I want to sell five pairs of knit socks, two sweaters, and six pairs of gloves this week since winter is coming up." If you can, answer these questions:

    o Who will be involved with this goal?

    o What is it that you want to accomplish?

    o Is there a specific location where

> this will take place?
> - What time frame do you have in mind?
> - What are the requirements or the constraints that are involved?
> - What are the specific reasons or the purpose of this goal?
> - What are the benefits of this goal?

- Measurable. This will fall in line with your "specific" goal as well. Instead of saying "sell lots of items this month", make it a measurable number: "Sell twenty pairs of socks before winter." Consider other types of goals as well:
    - Get 100 views on the blog tomorrow.
    - Get fifteen new customers this week.
    - Make five new pairs of socks by the end of the week.
- Achievable or attainable. You can attain almost any reasonable goal as long as you set the necessary steps to achieve it. Make sure that you have the right mindset as well. When you begin to realize that you are worthy of these goals, you will be able to set a reasonable long term goal with attainable short terms goals.

- Realistic. In order for a goal to be realistic, it must represent something that you are able to work toward and willing to work toward as well. Remember that just because you can do something, it doesn't mean that you will. You know yourself well, which makes you the perfect person to set these goals for yourself. If you want to make a goal which states that you will "refurbish and set up a listing for a vintage record player by tomorrow night," think long and hard about if you have the ability and desire to get it done in time. If you set a large amount of these goals, and are unable to achieve them, you will find yourself being more and more unsatisfied about this whole experience.

- Time bound or timely. Your goals should always have some type of time restraint. It should be built on a set time frame. If there isn't a time frame in mind, there aren't enough constraints on the goal to achieve it in a timely manner. The reason for having a goal like this is to give your unconscious mind a reason to work toward a goal with an anchor.

Do you have a "call to action" on your website or on your social media pages?
A "call to action" is the instruction that you give your visitor, reader, or potential customer. These can include:

- Call now.
- Click here to find out more.
- Visit our eBay listing.
- Visit my eBay profile for more information.
- Subscribe to our newsletter.

The "call to action" itself should be short at sweet. Don't make it too longwinded or elaborate. The attention span of most internet viewers are short. You want to be able to catch their attention and guide them in the right direction: to your eBay listing, to your subscription button, toward the shopping cart, etc. There are basically around eight different CTAs that you can have for your online business:

1. The "Sharing" Button. This is the most simple type of call to action. It is the "share to Facebook, Twitter, Pinterest, etc." button seen over images in a post or at the beginning of an article. These are wonderful because they require little to no commitment from your visitors. Place them in spots that appear to be common sense: landing pages, blog posts, articles, videos, etc. However, there is a fine line between using a few sharing buttons and plastering them all over your site. If your visitor can't hover their cursor over any section of your website without finding one, you've gone a bit too far.

2. Form Submission. These are used to gather information about your visitors. You use this information to customize their experience or to add their information to a contact database. It is critical to place a button at the end of a form submission which gives them more than just a "submit" button. Consider trading something with them: a guide, a handout, an infographic, etc. Visitors will be more likely to give you their contact information (first & last name, and email address, for example) if they can tangibly get something out of it. I like to automatically add my Ebay buyers to my list and offer a free gift on my listing. This way I am being paid to create a list of people that I can market to in the future.

3. "Read More". If you display a content feed of any kind, you can post a "Read More" CTA in order to tempt visitors to click on distinct and specific posts. This will limit the amount of information on a feed, allow you to show more posts on a feed, and can ensure that the actual posts get specific views. When this happens, you'll be able to see which posts get the most views. You can further enhance the content that you put out on your site using this information.

4. Promoting an Event. This is fairly self-explanatory. These are the "register for the event" buttons or the "mark your calendar" buttons. Some online

business owners place them on their home page. Consider placing one on the same page as their receipt or on their login page.

5. Lead Generation. This type of CTA is one which leads visitors to your website.

6. Lead Nurturing. This is the CTA that will take those leads and nurture them in order to entice them to be loyal customers. This means free trails or product demos. This may also mean free handouts, and other types of freebees that could bring your potential customers back.

7. Product Discovery. Let's say someone stumbles onto your website before they find your eBay page. You want to turn these visitors into customers. This can be done by making it easy for them to find your products. This CTA doesn't have to be fancy. A simple text stating "Thank you for visiting, have you seen..." would work just fine.

8. Closing the Sale. After all of the CTAs, the last one is the button that leads them to buy your product. This could be the button which leads to your eBay listing or to your shopping card.

Call to actions are important because these are the buttons and/or prompts which guide your potential customers in the right direction. You want to be able to entice them (give them little tidbits) to lead them to your product pages. However, you don't want to give them so much that they feel as though they no longer need your product. Effective CTAs try to catch the different types of audiences that stumble across your website or your post. They are able to generate those random visits into leads and product sales. Don't just slap a "buy now" button on your website and expect it to work flawlessly. They are a tad more complex than a simple button. You also have to consider CTA placement, color, text, phrasing, etc.

Just like with any other type of tool or design on your promotional sites, make sure that you are setting goals and playing around with different types of colors, shapes, and phrasing in order to find the perfect match for your website. You may not receive the same type of reception for your CTA as a similar website due to your audience and your products. Visit your favorite sites and take notes on how they use their CTAs and mimic what you think would work best for your site(s).

Chapter Eight: Money Magnet Mindset

A positive mindset is a powerful thing to have when in any business setting, whether it is from your corner office on the 100th floor or if it is in your home office, with a cat in your lap. If you look into the stories of any millionaire, 90% of them share this in common, proving that positive attitudes and optimism can be a deciding factor in success.

Let's first talk about what types of things should be thinking about besides money. Business is more than just money. In order to thrive in business, you need to be able to focus on three things:

- What are your values and assets?
- How can you focus and control your energy?
- Are you growing as an individual as your company is growing?
- Are you providing value and quality for your customer?

Your Values and Assets

Money is a type of asset but it won't be the asset that is the most critical. Your most significant asset is time. In order to be a good businessman – or woman – you're going to have to learn how to manage your time well.

There are many different methods for time management and each of them have a couple things in common:

- A planner of some kind to record your schedule. Most people keep a digital calendar handy on their smart phone, laptops, and tablets. The great thing about that technology is that they can all sync together so you will always be up- to- date on the latest changes in your schedule. Some people prefer the old school method of having a hardcopy planner. These come in a variety of different styles (monthly, weekly, daily, journal, binder, bound, etc.) which can suit almost any lifestyle. The great thing about hardcopy planners is that there have been studies done and publications which state that the act of writing something down triggers a signal in your cerebral cortex which actively engages your mind to pay more attention and remember more details. One example is in Henriette Anne Klauser's book, "Write It Down, Make It Happen" (http://www.henrietteklauser.com/_books/_writeitdown/index.htm). Speaking of which…

- Daily task list. Writing down a daily task list (no matter what format you choose) has been proven helpful for busy business owners all around the world. This is a practice that can be seen in almost every country from schools to multimillion dollar corporations because it works. Writing down a "to-do list" – or even a "not-to-do list" – has kept millions of people organized, on time, and productive for years.

In addition to your assets, your values are also important in business. This is a large part of what makes your brand special. You are setting out to create or refurbish products that will benefit your clientele. Putting in your best work into each of these products ensures that you can stand behind it without worrying about the customer's satisfaction.

Control and Focus

Taking control of your goals and moving forward is one of the best ways to ensure that you will have a thriving business in the future. Your business will work best when you are improving on your product and producing quality products. That means that you need to focus on being present while you are creating, in addition to improving on your craft. Like your profit, your improvement levels should always be rising.

Remember to also take control and responsibility of your actions. You are the face of your company. Because of this the business is yours and you must fix what goes wrong. This is your job. If the company falls apart, the employees will most likely leave, but you will still be there working on putting it back together and building it up again.

In addition to that, you're going to need to look at how you spend your money. It's not just about you anymore. If you think spending and saving money for a family is difficult, wait until you have to save that money for a company. Saving money in general is a different lifestyle. If you continue to spend unnecessary amounts of money, it won't just be you or your family that will have trouble. It will be everyone who relies on your company to save money. If you won't have employees, it probably won't be different than how you normally spend money, unless this is your sole income.

Growing as an Individual is as Important as Growing Your Business

Growing is important for your company and your business but it is just as important for yourself and your mindset. It might even be more important to help your mind grow because it will inevitably lead to your business growing in size.

Reading is one of the best ways that you can keep your mind sharp. Read voraciously. Read as much as you can. Read fiction and non-fiction. Read books that help you with business and books that help you with your craft. Reading books outside of your field is also helpful. It can aid you in thinking innovatively. Innovation breeds in an environment that nurtures creativity and in a place where you can meld different ideas together. Ideas that you wouldn't normally fit together. Innovation can come from the most surprising places after all. Learning new things (new ideas, new techniques, and new concepts) will keep you and your business in good shape.

After learning and reading, you'll need to be able to refresh your brain. Consider meditation as a great way to renew your mind. Letting your mind rest is vital to staying vigilant and healthy. Proper sleep and relaxation lets your mind organize the thoughts in your head. Your brain is bombarded with information and data all day long. When we don't get enough sleep, we don't give our brains enough time to process all of that data.

The Importance of Having a Positive Money Magnet Mindset

Now that we've talked about the mindset of an entrepreneur and how it is more than just thinking about money – it is a lifestyle change – let's focus on the positive. Specifically, optimism and its place in business.

Having a positive attitude means that you respond positively, make a positive influence on others, and perform actions which people would consider positive. When you act positively, people around you do the same as well. That means that when you respond in a positive way, it influences positive actions. You can say that the opposite is true as well. When you act negatively, it instigates negative reactions from others.

Unfortunately, there will be times when you won't want to act in a positive way. There will be times when not everything goes according to plan. When that happens, keep some of these things in mind:

- **Don't just react to things, be proactive as well.** When you only react to what is going on around you instead of being proactive in your life, you can feel like you're losing control of your life. Since you've already begun the process of starting your own business (either as your sole income or as a side job), you've already started to be proactive. Don't lose the momentum now. Continue to be proactive. This is your business. Don't be content with the small stream of organic customers that you run across. Instead, go out and market yourself. Market for those other customers.

- **Learn the benefits of being flexible and going with the flow.** While it is important to make things happen and be proactive, you still need to be flexible. With every plan, make sure that you have a bit of a back- up plan set up so that you can catch yourself if your plan fails. I hate to be the bearer of bad news but early on, you'll find that a lot of plans will fail. This is why it is important to be flexible. If you're too rigid, you will get disgruntled and disappointed easily. Too much disappointment can ruin anyone's attitude. So instead of viewing these failures for what they are, think of them as learning opportunities.

- **Keep your mind open.** An open mind is what leads to possibilities and new opportunities.

- **Don't be afraid of dreaming big.** Dreaming big might seem like the opposite of SMART Goals, but there is a distinctive difference. You can have both. While your goal may be to move a certain amount of product each month, you can still dream about owning your own successful business with a storefront someday. Don't limit your daydreaming to realistic constraints. If everyone only dreamt of realistic "dreams", we would not have the types of innovations that we have had in the past.

- **Find happy incentives**. Figure out what motivates you. If you're still early on in this business, you probably still know. If you've been in this for a while, you might be a bit jaded. Whenever you feel that pang of negativity, think back to why you started doing this in the first place. Discover what motivates you. Keep your values in mind when you consider your motivations for work. Does this include financial success? Is it stability? Do your motivations lie in creating a product that will make someone happy? Do you like to bring life to vintage items that still have life in them?

- **Be confident in your actions and don't be afraid of being bold.** There is a difference – though it can sometimes be a fine line – between being confident and being arrogant. The difference between the two is the same difference between being aggressive and being compassionate. When you are arrogant, it is an external show of emotions while being confident is an internal process. While both of these have roots in high self-esteem and a strong belief in what they can accomplish, confidence is inherently more positive. People who are confident are strong and admirable. They can easily overcome fear and uncertainty. The main difference between the two lies in these differences:

    o Confident people have a positive attitude.

    o Communication with arrogant people isn't pleasant.

    o Arrogant people look past you while confident people can sincerely look into your eyes and make strong – yet comfortable – eye contact.

- Condescending remarks toward others.

- Arrogant people have strained or painful relationships with others.

- Healthy self-perception. Confident people know how to handle their own weaknesses while arrogant people don't think they have shortcomings.

Be confident. Believe in yourself. When you have a strong sense of self and when you are confident in yourself, you will begin looking at the world in a more positive light and that is how success is created.

- **Surround yourself with positive people.** Positive interactions beget positive attitudes and more positive actions. If you surround yourself with negative people, you will find yourself thinking negatively. It is said that opposites attract and while that may be true, it isn't necessarily healthy. Remember that it only takes one person who is toxic to ruin a whole campaign. The morale of the people around you hinge on everyone people around us. Also, when you fill your social and professional circle with people who are goal-oriented, successful, and happy, you can learn from each other. You can pick up their habits and add them to your repertoire. Certain behaviors aren't just natural to us. Some of them can be learned. Positive habits are just an example of those types of learned behaviors.

- **Accept the challenge of being a businessperson.** Starting your own business is a scary endeavor because different markets can be incredibly fickle. However, if you accept this challenge, it can be one of the most rewarding experiences of your life. Even if you take a stab at it and fail, you will learn a plethora of incredible, life-changing lessons. This journey will help mold you into a more well-rounded and intelligent person.

- **Take a deep breath.** We will always find ourselves in a spot where we are thinking negatively. When this happens, go through these steps:

    o *Slow down and take a deep breath. Negative reactions are normally gut reactions to bad situations. Don't dwell on those bad situations. Take a moment and clear your mind. Even the simple act of breathing in deeply and slowly, then breathing out slowly, can trigger a reaction in your prefrontal cortex that will help you become more rational.*

    o *Be mindful of those around you and of your actions. Use specific words and actions in order to try and change how you feel.*

- *Think before you say or do anything. Words spoken in anger or negatively can have a powerful reaction.*

- *Be grateful for what you do have. We are all lucky. For the most part, we have food on the table and a roof over our heads. For that we should all be grateful. Reflecting on the small positive things that happen to you is just one way to put everything back in perspective.*

- *Do something good for someone else. Charitable acts have a way of lifting up spirits.*

- *Set up some ambitious goals. Keep the big picture in mind. If you are bummed about a small failure, don't focus on the failure. Use it as a learning opportunity and think about how you can use that lesson toward your big goal.*

- *Don't fall into the trap of thinking negative thoughts about yourself. It is an easy trap to fall into and it can just as easily spiral out of control. Starting your own business on eBay – your own online business – is difficult. Cut yourself some slack, take a deep breath, and look forward.*

- *Fake it until you make it. It is possible to fake the mindset of thinking positively until that is how you actually feel – especially in short term bouts of negative thinking.*

Are you providing Value to Your Customers?

I have now been in business for many years, and in the beginning I had the same goal as many of you will currently have. To make money.

As time went on I began to learn from successful people, and the more successful people I spoke to, the more I realized this to be true.

Look after your customers, focusing on providing great quality products, great quality information and great customer service. The rest will simply fall into place.

It sounds really simple, but it wasn't until I implemented this in my businesses that I learnt how powerful this really is! Trust me!

Lastly…

I hope that this book has been of some help to you and your business goals, we have now reached the end of our EBay adventure.

However, I want to provide you with some free bonuses to help you with your next step and provide as much value to you as I can.

For purchasing this book, I want to give you access to my free 5 part video course on making money online. This video course will walk you step by step through 5 business models you can start without any prior technical skills, knowledge or even capital!

If you would like to enrol on this then please visit the site below:

www.tycoonfactory.com/freecourse

Please remember the key to success is to take massive action, so get out there and DO IT!

If you have enjoyed this, you might also be interested in some of the articles on my blog.

Feel free to check this out at:

www.tycoonfactory.com

and sign up for a second free gift there !

Thank you and good luck!

Printed in Great Britain
by Amazon